KNIGHTS
OF THE
ROUND
TABLE

15

First published in Great Britain by
CAXTON EDITIONS
an imprint of
The Caxton Book Company,
16 Connaught Street,
Marble Arch, London, W2 2AF.

ISBN 1 84067 027 4

A copy of the CIP data for this book is available from the British Library upon request.

With grateful thanks to Helen Courtney

Created and produced for Caxton Editions by
FLAME TREE PUBLISHING,
a part of The Foundry Creative Media Company Ltd,
Crabtree Hall, Crabtree Lane,
Fulham, London, SW6 6TY.

Printed in Singapore by Star Standard Industries Pte. Ltd.

HEADstart

KNIGHTS
OF THE
ROUND
TABLE

MAUREEN HILL

CAXTON EDITIONS

Contents

Introduction

The stories of the Knights of the Round Table are legends. Like many legends they are a mixture of fact and fiction, of truth and fantasy, of reality and magic.

King Arthur was the leader of the Knights of the Round Table. The legend of Arthur is thought to have been based on a real leader of the Britons in the sixth century. This Arthur fought against the invading Anglo Saxons and had his court at Caerleon, on the border between England and Wales. He is also believed to have fought abroad, perhaps in France, against the might of the Roman army.

The first mention of Arthur is in a Welsh tale written at the very beginning of the seventh century. Later on, in the eleventh century, tales began to be told of Arthur's knights. The

stories have been retold over the years and have developed into some of the best-known legends of all time. Tales of the Knights of the Round Table can be found all across Europe, especially in the medieval tales of France and Italy. The tales are full of

action, adventure, heroism, love, betrayal, drama and magic.

Merlin and Arthur

The story of the Knights of the Round Table really begins with Merlin. It was his vision of a great king who would free the Ancient Britons from invaders and enemy armies that created Arthur.

Merlin was a magician. He was brought up in Wales by his grandfather and from a very young age he had the gift of being able to see into the future. He also had magic powers, among which was the power to change shape.

Merlin knew that the parents of the future king would be Uther Pendragon, king of the Britons, and his wife, the beautiful Ygraine. The only problem was that Ygraine was married to Gorlois, friend of Uther.

Uther was madly in love with Ygraine but she loved her husband. One night, when Gorlois was away from his castle at Tintagel, Merlin used his magic powers to change Uther's appearance. He made him look like Gorlois. The deception was so good that even Ygraine was fooled into thinking Uther was Gorlois.

Uther spent one night with Ygraine during which she conceived a son, whom she named Arthur. Later that year Gorlois was killed in battle, and Uther and Ygraine married and lived together in Camelot. However, Uther had been so desperate to spend the time with Ygraine before their marriage that he had made a bargain – that Merlin could take the child when he was one year old and raise him in secret.

Arthur's Childhood

When Arthur was one year old, Merlin took him away from Uther and Ygraine. This was in part due to the bargain made with Uther and partly to protect him from enemies who might have harmed him.

Merlin took the young Arthur to the home of a country knight named Sir Hector. Sir Hector was simple, honest and good. Merlin persuaded Sir Hector and his wife that the child was an orphan and asked them to raise him along with their own children.

So Arthur stayed with Sir Hector and his family. Sir Hector taught him all about archery, horsemanship, jousting and fighting battles. Every so often Merlin would visit to teach the young Arthur reading, writing, arithmetic, science, art and a little magic!

Arthur grew up alongside Sir Hector's son, Kay. As boys there was a friendly rivalry between Arthur and Kay. Kay was a few years older than Arthur and so would inherit his father's title and become a knight. Arthur also wanted to become a knight, but as the younger brother his role was to be squire to Kay, attending him and helping him prepare for jousts and battles.

Although Arthur had a very happy childhood, he longed for adventure and was determined to be something more than just a squire to his older brother. He was strong and capable of beating Kay, but was wise enough to let Kay win, knowing how much defeat by Arthur would hurt his pride.

One winter's day Merlin arrived at Sir Hector's home with the news that Uther Pendragon was dead. As Arthur was still only a boy, Ygraine ruled alone.

The Sword in the Stone

For several years Ygraine led the Britons, but there were many problems and threats of war. Merlin decided that although Arthur was only 16 years old, it was time for him to become king.

One Christmas there appeared in the churchyard of the castle of Camelot a huge block of marble. Set into the stone was a beautiful sword, and below the sword there was an inscription in gold letters:

Whoever can draw this sword is the rightful king of all Britain

News of this amazing stone spread and several kings travelled from neighbouring kingdoms to try their luck at retrieving the sword from the stone. Not one of them succeeded.

Ygraine and the kings decided to hold a great tournament and to award the crown to the winner of the tournament.

Sir Hector came with his sons Kay and Arthur. Arthur, acting as squire to Kay, was responsible for making sure that Kay had all his equipment for the tournament – breastplate, shield, helmet, lance and sword.

'Where's my sword, Arthur?' called Kay from his horse as he was about to enter the tournament. Arthur had forgotten it. In desperation he ran to their lodgings but the house was closed – everyone had gone to watch the tournament. Arthur ran past the churchyard and noticed the sword in the stone. Not stopping to read the inscription he grabbed the sword and ran back to the tournament.

Sir Hector recognised the sword at once and so did several others. Everyone demanded that Arthur show them just how he took the sword from the stone.

They all went to the churchyard and Arthur replaced the sword into the stone. The kings tried once again to draw it from the stone, but failed. Arthur stepped forward and pulled it out with ease. The crowd roared, 'Long live King Arthur!'.

Arthur Adventurous

Arthur was very young when he came to the throne. He had to earn the respect of his fellow knights – and he was called to do so quite soon after he was crowned.

Several of the kings who had been present when he drew the sword from the stone were not content to accept Arthur as King of Britain. They plotted to overthrow him and divide up his kingdom. Arthur led his knights into battle against them. He fought bravely and defeated the enemies of Britain.

Soon after this battle, one of the kings who had supported Arthur asked for help when his kingdom was attacked by bandits. Arthur marched to help King Lodegrance, but his reputation was so great that the bandits fled when they heard he was coming. King Lodegrance was very grateful and held a feast in Arthur's honour. At the feast, Arthur met and fell in love with Guinevere, Lodegrance's daughter.

Despite his love for Guinevere, Arthur had to return to Camelot. Here he was faced with a call from Brittany in France, to help kill a monstrous giant that was terrorising the countryside. The giant had killed thousands and captured and imprisoned the Duke and Duchess of Brittany.

Arthur sailed for Brittany and tracked down the giant. He found him camped in a forest preparing a meal of roasted children. Arthur attacked him in fury and disgust. He attacked with such force that as he slashed at the giant's leg his sword broke in two. As the giant toppled Arthur cut off his head with the broken sword.

The Sword from the Lake

Merlin took Arthur to the shores of a lake. As they looked across its surface, a hand appeared holding a sword in a beautifully jewelled 'scabbard', or holder. Then a woman emerged from the lake and walked across the surface of the water to a small island. 'The Lady of the Lake,' said Merlin. 'Take that boat and we can row out to her.'

When Arthur and Merlin reached the Lady she gave the sword to Arthur, telling him it was an enchanted sword made only for him. She parted

from them with a warning. 'Arthur, when the time comes for you to leave this life you must return this sword to the water from which it came. If it is not returned it will rust and rot away and so will the memory of your name.'

Merlin told Arthur that the sword was called Excalibur and that it could cut through iron and steel and would never break. But he also told him to value the scabbard more than the sword, for as long as Arthur wore the scabbard he would never lose one drop of blood.

Once Merlin had seen to it that Arthur had Excalibur to defend and protect him, he knew it was time to leave his precious king. He felt his powers fading, and knew that while Arthur had many glorious days ahead, he would also suffer many difficulties and pains.

Merlin retreated to a cave to watch Arthur in his visions. Many people say that he remains there to this day.

Arthur and Guinevere

Arthur had fallen in love with Guinevere when he first saw her at the feast in her father's kingdom. She loved him too, and they planned to marry on Midsummer's Day.

Arthur and Guinevere could not have been happier, but before he left Merlin had warned Arthur that their marriage would end tragically. Arthur would not listen, and for the first time he was angry with Merlin, dismissing his fears and advice.

Preparations for the wedding went ahead and soon Camelot was filled with visitors, colourful tents and flags, and flowers. Kings and knights came from far and wide to take part in the celebrations, which were to take the form of a grand tournament, lasting seven days.

Arthur and Guinevere looked the perfect couple as they took their marriage vows. The crowds cheered, pleased that their king had found such a lovely queen.

Lodegrance sent them a huge and magnificent round table as a wedding present. The table was made of oak and was large enough to seat over a hundred people. The moment he saw it Arthur knew that it would play an important part in his dream of gathering together a band of the best, most chivalrous knights. He declared that those knights at the tournament who displayed the most skill and courage would win a seat at the Round Table.

The Best Knight

By the seventh day of the tournament to celebrate Arthur and Guinevere's marriage, nearly all the seats at the Round Table had been filled. As each knight took his place his name appeared magically in gold letters on his seat. Soon there were only two seats left.

A strange knight rode into Camelot and asked to join the tournament. His visor was down, covering his face and he wore no symbols to show who he was. He said would not reveal his name until he proved himself. Arthur cherished openness and honesty, but Guinevere persuaded him to give the knight a chance.

The stranger took on the best and strongest knights from the Round Table, and he defeated them all. He then removed his helmet and knelt down before Arthur and

said, 'My lord, I am Lancelot du Lac, son of King Ban of Benwick'.

Lancelot then turned to thank Guinevere for persuading Arthur to allow him to fight, but as he looked into her eyes they fell in love with each other. Both Lancelot and Guinevere were sad for they knew that their love could never be.

Lancelot took his place at the Round Table. His name, too, appeared in gold letters, but on the seat next to his appeared the words 'Siege Perilous' or 'dangerous seat'. As yet, no knight was fit to take such a seat. It was reserved for the perfect knight and it was to remain empty for many years to come.

The Fellowship of the Round Table

The list of the Knights of the Round Table is a long one. It includes the twin knights Sir Balin and Sir Balan, Arthur's foster brother Sir Kay, Sir Bors, Sir Agravain, Sir Melligrance, Sir Bedevere (who was with Arthur in his last great battle), Sir Perceval, Sir Pellinore and his son Sir Lamorak, Sir Lucan, Sir Tor, and many, many more. When one knight died, either killed in battle or from old age, his name would fade from his chair and be replaced by the name of another worthy knight.

Each year in Camelot the Knights of the Round Table swore an oath to obey the laws of the Fellowship. These were to fight fairly for truth and honour; never to do battle for selfish ends or for worldly goods; to give help to those in distress; to show mercy; and to respect their brother Knights of the Round Table.

It was a knight's duty to take part in adventures and quests. Every Knight of the Round Table took part in some exciting or noble adventure, whether it was Sir Yvain who fought the Black Knight and married the Lady of the Fountain, Sir Beaumains who killed the Red Knight and saved the Lady Lynette, or Sir Gawain and his brother Sir Gaheris who were for some time trapped with Sir Marholt in the Land of Stones by sorceresses.

Sir Gawain and the Green Knight

Arthur and his Knights were enjoying a feast to celebrate the New Year, when into the great hall at Camelot strode an enormous green man, carrying an enormous axe and a holly bush.

This Green Knight told Arthur how the fame of the Knights of the Round Table had spread far and wide. He set down a challenge before the company. His challenge was that, using his great green axe, a Knight of the Round Table would dare chop off his great green head. There was one condition, though. This was that the following New Year's Day, the Green Knight be allowed to do exactly the same to the knight.

Sir Gawain accepted the challenge. He swung the great green axe and lopped off the head of the Green Knight. To everyone's astonishment the Green Knight did not fall, but picked up his head and walked out of Camelot. As he left, the mouth in the head said, 'remember your promise, Sir Gawain. You must seek me out next New Year's Day'.

Sir Gawain was an honourable knight, and would not break his promise, although it meant certain death. He set out several days before Christmas the following year to seek the Green Knight.

After journeying for many days he came to the land where the Green Knight lived. He was given shelter in the castle of a local lord. The lord went hunting every day, but realising Sir Gawain was tired from his travels and would prefer to stay indoors he made a curious bargain. The bargain was that the lord and Gawain would exchange whatever they had managed to 'hunt' that day.

On the first day Gawain was approached by the wife of the lord, who kissed him. In the evening the lord returned and Gawain gave the lord the kiss in return for the stag he had caught. On the second day the lord's wife gave Gawain two kisses, which were later exchanged for the lord's trophies from the hunt.

On the third day Gawain was given three kisses and a green girdle that the lord's wife said would protect him from harm. Thinking of his coming meeting with the Green Knight Gawain kept the girdle but gave the lord the kisses.

The next day was New Year's Day and Gawain set out for the Green Knight's temple. There the Green Knight came to meet him.

Gawain knelt down, put his head on a block of stone and waited for the blow from the giant axe. Twice the Green Knight brought the axe down with a tremendous swoop, only to stop at the last minute. 'Come on, get on with it,' said a trembling Sir Gawain.

The third time, the Green Knight brought the axe down and nicked the skin of Gawain's neck. 'Get up, Sir Gawain,' said the Knight. When Gawain stood up he saw not the Green Knight, but the lord with whom he had stayed. 'You are a virtuous knight. You told me honestly of the kisses my wife gave you. But you were not honest about the girdle. That is why I cut you.'

Gawain felt ashamed, and said, 'I deserve to die for being so cowardly'.

But the lord replied, 'you made a small mistake and you treasure your own life. Those are no great crimes. Go on your way, brave knight'.

Sir Lancelot

There are many tales of Sir Lancelot, for he was the bravest and the best of the Knights of the Round Table for many years. He was surpassed by only one knight, and that was the knight who was to occupy the 'Siege Perilous'.

One of Lancelot's most important adventures involved the Holy Grail. The Holy Grail was the cup that Jesus Christ drank from at the Last Supper, and which was used to collect the blood from his wounds. The Grail had been kept by the Fisher Kings for hundreds of years, until a terrible tragedy befell the Fisher King Pellam.

Pellam was injured in the thigh by a blow from a lance, and at the moment he received his injury, the Castle of Corbenic, the Fisher Kings' home, had fallen into ruins and the whole of the surrounding land had become a bleak wasteland.

Lancelot learned of the injured Fisher King and of the Wasteland, and set out to try to help heal and restore both of them. He travelled to Castle Corbenic where he was made very welcome.

'We have been expecting you. Come in, noble knight,' said King Pelles, son of King Pellam. He led Lancelot to a feast laid out among the ruins of the castle. After he had eaten, a beautiful woman came in carrying a golden bowl. The woman knelt and prayed, then carried the bowl away. Pelles told Lancelot that he had glimpsed the Holy Grail.

That night Lancelot slept in a room in a ruined tower of Castle Corbenic. When he awoke the next morning, he found the young woman that had carried the Holy Grail lying beside him. She told him she was Elaine, Pelles' daughter, and that together they had made a child who would be the perfect knight and would one day heal the Fisher King.

Sir Galahad

After his night with Elaine, Lancelot left Castle Corbenic and returned to Camelot. But when Guinevere learned of what had happened, she was very jealous and sent Lancelot away.

In his unhappiness Lancelot wandered for many months, and became quite ill. Eventually, Elaine found him in a forest and helped him back to physical and mental health. For many years they lived happily together with their son Galahad in a castle called Joyous Garde.

Lancelot taught Galahad everything he knew about the skills and duties of a knight, and his grandfather, King Pelles, taught him the secrets of the Fisher King and the Holy Grail.

Back in Camelot a new inscription appeared on the Siege Perilous:

This is the seat of the perfect knight, Sir Galahad

Knights from the Round Table were sent to find this young knight.

Eventually a knight called Perceval found Galahad and Lancelot in Joyous Garde. There was much rejoicing in Camelot at the arrival of Galahad and the return of Lancelot.

No sooner had Galahad been knighted and taken his place at the Round Table than a dove with a golden bowl appeared before the Fellowship. A voice from the air said, 'I am the Holy Grail. Only the best may find me. With me the perfect knight will heal the injured Fisher King and the Wasteland'.

Each knight in turn swore to seek the Holy Grail, however dangerous the quest might be.

The Quest for the Holy Grail

The day after the vision of the Grail appeared to the Knights of the Round Table, they all rode out in search of it.

After a year, many knights returned, having failed in their quest. Many knights did not return at all, having died in the attempt. Soon only five knights were unaccounted for: Gawain, Lancelot, Bors, Perceval and Galahad.

Gawain returned some months later, followed by Lancelot, who told Arthur that he had glimpsed the Holy Grail but had been unable to capture it.

Bors returned shortly afterwards and his tale was marvellous. He told how he, Galahad and Perceval had encountered King Pellam, lying injured on a bed. A table then appeared on which was the Holy Grail. Galahad took the Grail and with it healed the Fisher King.

Immediately Castle Corbenic reformed itself into the wonderful place it had once been. Looking out of the windows, Bors could see that the Wasteland was no more. In its place was a rich, fruitful and colourful land.

'But what of Sir Perceval and Sir Galahad?' asked Arthur.

'Perceval parted from me in the forest, determined to seek out a holy man and spend his days in holy contemplation,' said Sir Bors.

'But as for Galahad,' continued Bors, 'when the Wasteland and the Fisher King were both healed, the Lady of the Lake appeared and took him to Avalon'. The knights were sad, for although they knew that only the purest of heart went to Avalon, they also knew they would never see Galahad in this life again.

Morgan le Fay

Arthur's half-sister, Morgan le Fay, was a sorceress, and a very powerful one at that. She had always hated Arthur and had often plotted his downfall. At first she had hidden her true feelings and had appeared to be Arthur's friend, but soon Arthur saw how she really felt about him and no longer trusted her.

Just before Arthur and Guinevere's marriage, and before Merlin disappeared, Morgan sent one of her maids with a present for her younger brother's wife-to-be. It was a beautiful cloak, made of the finest fabrics and decorated with precious jewels.

Arthur was delighted and could not wait for Guinevere to try it on. Merlin was suspicious. He knew of Morgan's skills and of her hatred for her brother. As the maid held the cloak up for Arthur and Guinevere to admire, Merlin suggested she might like to put it on to display it better.

'Oh no, it is much too fine a garment for me. It is only fit for a queen,' replied the maid in a shaking voice.

'Please try it on,' said Arthur.

'Oh really, I couldn't!' exclaimed the maid, avoiding Arthur's gaze.

'I order you to put it on,' commanded Arthur.

The maid did so and the cloak burst into flames, burning the maid with it.

Although Morgan le Fay had failed this time, she continued to plot against Arthur. Gradually, she made some allies within the Fellowship of the Round Table.

Mordred

ordred was Arthur's nephew, the son of another of his half-sisters and brother to Sir Gawain, Sir Gareth and Sir Gaheris. He was also a Knight of the Round Table and an enemy of Arthur.

Arthur trusted Mordred at first, just as he had trusted Morgan le Fay, and believed him to be an honourable knight. Mordred was secretly plotting with Morgan a way to bring about Arthur's downfall and take the throne himself.

ordred found an opportunity in the love between Guinevere and Lancelot. Although Lancelot had married Elaine, he continued to love Guinevere best. Everyone in Camelot except Arthur knew of their love, and although it was innocent, Mordred devised a way to make it look as if Guinevere and Lancelot had been cheating on Arthur behind his back. He tricked Lancelot into Guinevere's bedroom and then called Arthur to witness his presence there.

Arthur was distraught – the penalty for unfaithfulness to the king was death. Guinevere was to be burned at the stake. Arthur could not make an exception; he must act according to the laws of the land.

Lancelot could not bear to see Guinevere die, and so mounted a daring rescue with some knights who believed Arthur had acted too quickly and judged too harshly. In the fight to rescue Guinevere, Lancelot killed several of his old companions, including Gawain's brothers Gareth and Gaheris. Lancelot and Guinevere fled to Joyous Garde.

When Gawain learned that his old friend had killed his two brothers, he swore vengeance on Lancelot and requested Arthur's help to do so.

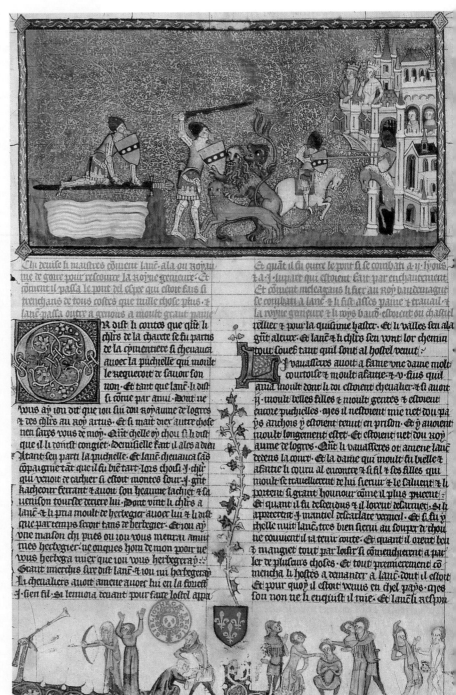

The Death of Arthur

Gawain's pledge of vengeance on Lancelot split the Fellowship of the Round Table. Some knights sided with Gawain and Arthur while others joined Lancelot in his castle at Joyous Garde.

Arthur left Mordred in charge while he led his knights to attack Lancelot. But while Arthur was away dreadful news came from Camelot. Mordred had taken the throne.

On Arthur's return to Camelot a great battle took place. Arthur met Mordred face-to-face and he ran his spear through his evil heart. As he fell, Mordred caught Arthur a fatal blow on his head.

The dying Arthur called to Sir Bedevere to take his sword Excalibur and throw it into the lake. Bedevere took the sword and soon returned to Arthur's side. 'What did you see?' said Arthur.

'Nothing,' replied Bedevere.

'Then you have not done as I asked. Do so now.'

Bedevere went again to the lake's edge. This time he took the sword from where he had hidden it but could not bring himself to throw it into the water.

He returned and Arthur asked him again what he had seen.

'Nothing,' he replied.

'Please Bedevere, do as I ask so that I may live on,' pleaded Arthur.

This time Bedevere threw the sword into the lake, and marvelled to see a hand come out of the water, grasp it and take it below the waves.

He returned to Arthur and told him what he had seen. Arthur simply nodded and asked to be taken to the lake shore.

At the edge of the lake a small boat had appeared. In it stood the Lady of the Lake. Bedevere helped Arthur into the boat which then floated away, taking Arthur on his journey to Avalon.

Further Information

Places to Visit

Many places throughout Britain claim to be the site of Arthur's Camelot or to be the lake into which Excalibur was thrown. The following sites may be of interest:

Glastonbury, Wiltshire - it is claimed that Arthur's and Guinevere's bones are buried in the Abbey Church.

Glastonbury Tor - just outside the town of Glastonbury is an unusually shaped hill. Legend claims that the Holy Grail was buried here. On top of the hill is the ruined Chapel of St Michael. At the bottom of the hill is the Chalice Well.
For further information on the area contact Glastonbury Tourist Office.
Telephone: 01458 832954.

Tintagel Castle - Arthur's birthplace. Tintagel Castle, Tintagel, Cornwall, PL34 0HE.
Telephone: 01840 770328.

Further Reading

Knight, Dorling Kindersley, 1994.
The Adventures Of King Arthur And His Knights Of The Round Table by R.L. Green.
The Dark Is Rising (Series) by Susan Cooper.
The Lantern Bearers by Rosemary Sutcliff.
The Once and Future King by T. H. White – four books based on the life of King Arthur.
Castle, Dorling Kindersley, 1994.
The Road To Camlann by Rosemary Sutcliff.

Videos and CD Roms

The Sword In The Stone, Disney Video Series.
Camelot - a musical film of some of the tales of the Knights of the Round Table.

Britannia's Arthur Website - http://britannia.com/history/arthur - timeline, details of sites connected with Arthur, information about the real and the legendary Arthur.

these are the arms of certain knights of the round table bidden to seek the sangreal who departed on the quest whatever might befal but of those that thus departed these are the chiefest. sir gawaine of orkney. sir lancelot. sir hector de marys. sir bors. sir percival. and sir galahad

Picture Credits

The Bridgeman Art Library: pp. 8, 14, 17, 18, 20, 22, 24, 24-25, 28, 29, 30, 31, 33, 38, 39, 40, 41, 43(t), 43(b)
Christie's Images: pp. 12, 13, 14-15, 16, 19, 35
Mary Evans Picture Library: pp. 32
Visual Arts Library: pp. 10, 11, 21, 23, 26, 27, 34, 36, 37